THE OFFICIAL ANNUAL 2020

Written by Matt Joyce, Iain Pearce, Neil Perrett & Zoe Rundle
Designed by Chris Payne

A Grange Publication

© 2019. Published by Grange Communications Ltd., Edinburgh, under licence from AFC Bournemouth. Printed in the EU.

Photographs © Robin Jones, Amy Maidment, Getty Images

ISBN: 978-1-913034-14-6

CONTENTS

AFC BOURNEMOUTH SQUAD 2019/20

EDDIE HOWE
Manager

JASON TINDALL
Assistant Manager

1

ARTUR BORUC
Goalkeeper

12

AARON RAMSDALE
Goalkeeper

27

ASMIR BEGOVIC
Goalkeeper

42

MARK TRAVERS
Goalkeeper

2

SIMON FRANCIS
Defender

3

STEVE COOK
Defender

5

NATHAN AKE
Defender

11

CHARLIE DANIELS
Defender

15

ADAM SMITH
Defender

17

JACK STACEY
Defender

21

DIEGO RICO
Defender

25

JACK SIMPSON
Defender

26

LLOYD KELLY
Defender

33
CHRIS MEPHAM
Defender

4
DAN GOSLING
Midfielder

6
ANDREW SURMAN
Midfielder

8
JEFFERSON LERMA
Midfielder

10
JORDON IBE
Midfielder

14
ARNAUT DANJUMA
Midfielder

16
LEWIS COOK
Midfielder

19
JUNIOR STANISLAS
Midfielder

20
DAVID BROOKS
Midfielder

22
HARRY WILSON
Midfielder

24
RYAN FRASER
Midfielder

28
KYLE TAYLOR
Midfielder

29
PHILIP BILLING
Midfielder

36
MATT BUTCHER
Midfielder

38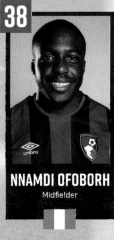
NNAMDI OFOBORH
Midfielder

53
GAVIN KILKENNY
Midfielder

7
JOSHUA KING
Forward

9
DOMINIC SOLANKE
Forward

13
CALLUM WILSON
Forward

54
ALEX DOBRE
Forward

SEASON 2018/19
IN NUMBERS

10
The Cherries kept 10 clean sheets in 2018/19, matching the previous best, set in 2016/17. They have kept 33 clean sheets in four seasons in the Premier League.

150
Goals from Ryan Fraser and Callum Wilson earned the Cherries a 2-0 win on the opening day of 2018/19 as Eddie Howe celebrated his 150th victory as manager of the Dorset club.

9
Callum Wilson scored nine goals away from home, finishing joint-third in the Premier League alongside Arsenal's Pierre-Emerick Aubameyang, Liverpool's Mo Salah and Crystal Palace's Wilfried Zaha. Ryan Fraser finished top of the away assists table with nine.

8
Nathan Ake missed just eight minutes of the Cherries' 3,420 minutes in the Premier League.

56
The Cherries scored 56 goals in 38 Premier League games in 2018/19, their best return in four seasons in the top flight.

500

The Cherries' 1-0 defeat by Fulham at Vitality Stadium in April was Eddie Howe's 500th game in management.

12

Ryan Fraser and Callum Wilson combined for 12 goals, a record for a 38-game season in the Premier League.

20

The Cherries took 20 points from their first ten games, their best return in a top-flight campaign.

14

Callum Wilson bagged 14 goals to win the Cherries' golden boot, while Ryan Fraser contributed the same number of assists.

200

Jordon Ibe's goal in the Cherries' 5-3 defeat at Crystal Palace on the final day of the season was the club's 200th goal in the Premier League.

5

The Cherries' 5-0 win at Brighton in April was their most emphatic away victory in the Premier League.

13

Victory over Tottenham in their final home game of the season was the Cherries' 13th of the campaign, their best return since they have been in the top flight.

Zero
A 3-3 draw at Luton in December 2008 saw the Cherries finally wipe out their 17-point deduction and move on to zero points during the Great Escape season.

Young
Long-serving right-back Neil Young made 429 league appearances between October 1994 and May 2008.

X-Ray
Matt Holland once played for the Cherries with a broken arm, a post-match x-ray revealing the midfielder had sustained the fracture.

White
Jimmy White is the club's youngest debutant having featured in a 3-1 win over Port Vale in April 1958 aged 15 years and 321 days.

Voisey
Bill Voisey started the Cherries' first game in the Football League, a 3-1 defeat at Swindon in August 1923.

Under-20s
Cherries defender Baily Cargill marked his debut for England under-20s by scoring in a 2-2 draw against Canada at Vitality Stadium in November 2014.

Teale
Defender Shaun Teale made 100 league appearances for the Cherries between January 1989 and July 1991 and was named player of the year in 1989/90 and 1990/91.

Stock
Brian Stock scored the first goal in a 3-0 win over Wrexham in the first game played at the developed Dean Court in November 2001 after the pitch had been turned 90 degrees.

Redknapp
Harry Redknapp became the first manager to guide the club to a title with a then-record 97 points seeing them win the old Third Division in 1986/87.

Quinn
Striker Jimmy Quinn was the Cherries' leading goalscorer in 1991/92 and briefly managed the club in 2008.

Pitman
Prolific frontman Brett Pitman led the goal charts as the Cherries gained promotion from League Two (2010) and League One (2013) and was crowned supporters' player of the year in 2009/10.

O'Driscoll
Midfielder Sean O'Driscoll starred in the club's 1986/87 Third Division title triumph and managed the club to Division Three play-off final glory against Lincoln City in 2002/03.

Northampton Town
The Cherries' 10-0 win against the Cobblers in 1939/40 – their biggest victory in the Football League – was expunged from the records when the season was cancelled following the outbreak of war.

AFC Bournemouth

The club's name since the early 1970s which replaced Bournemouth & Boscombe Athletic.

Busby

Sir Matt Busby, the legendary Man United manager, was a guest player for the Cherries during 1945/46.

Cutler

Reg Cutler almost caused the abandonment of the Cherries' 1956/57 FA Cup fourth round tie against Wolves when he crashed into the goalpost which led to the goal collapsing. After it had been repaired, Cutler scored the only goal to earn the Cherries one of their most famous cup wins.

Dean Court

The club's home ground since 1910 was named after the land owner JE Cooper-Dean JP who became club president.

Eyre

Roland 'Ron' Eyre remains the club's all-time leading goalscorer having netted 202 times in 302 games between January 1925 and May 1933.

Fletcher

Striker Steve Fletcher holds the club's appearance record having played 628 times in two spells between July 1992 and July 2007, and January 2009 and May 2013.

Graham

Striker Milton Graham opened the scoring during the Cherries' memorable 2-0 win over holders Manchester United in the third round of the FA Cup in January 1984.

Howe

A popular figure as a player, Eddie Howe is the club's most successful manager having led them from the depths of League Two to the Premier League in two spells.

International

Goalkeeper Tommy Godwin became the club's first full international when he lined up for Republic of Ireland in a 4-1 win over the Netherlands in Rotterdam in May 1956.

Jones

No fewer than ten players with the surname Jones have played for the Cherries – Andy Jones, Bryn Jones, David Jones, Gareth Jones, Glanville Jones, Jack Jones, Kenwyne Jones, Mickey Jones, Roger Jones, Steve Jones.

Kermorgant

Frenchman Yann Kermorgant bagged a hat-trick on his full debut for the Cherries in a 5-0 win against Doncaster in March 2014 and played a starring role as the club lifted the Championship title in 2014/15.

MacDougall

Revered striker Ted MacDougall is the club's post-war record leading marksman, having netted 119 goals in 198 league games in two spells.

Lincoln City

The Cherries triumphed 5-2 against the Imps to win the Division Three play-off final at the Millennium Stadium in Cardiff in May 2003.

FAMOUS KITS THROUGH THE YEARS

Join us as we take a look back through the most famous kits ever worn by the mighty Cherries!

EARLY DAYS

It's very rare to get any photos of our legendary striker Ron Eyre. But here's one, of course in black and white, because of the time! The Cherries actually wore red and white during this time – and wore those colours up until 1970!

'71

THE 70'S

Back in Ted MacDougall's era, the Cherries kits were far simpler than the red and black that Eddie Howe's side wear these days! No sponsors existed and there was no badge in place at all.

In 1971, when the striker scored his famous nine goals in an FA Cup game against Margate, there wasn't even any black on the shirt, with it being all red and having a white collar!

THE MILLENNIUM

A very young Jermain Defoe came on loan to Bournemouth at the start of the century and made quite the impact with supporters. The former England international scored in ten consecutive appearances, with the record being set away at Cambridge mid-way through the season!

The kit he wore to do it in maintained the black and red stripes which you see at Vitality Stadium today, but the crest is slightly different to the one that Eddie Howe's side don on their shirts now. Jermain himself would sometimes look like he was wearing a dress, the shirts were that baggy back then!

GREAT ESCAPE

There were tough times for AFC Bournemouth in the 2008/09 season, as the club just managed to stay in the Football League thanks to an 84th minute strike from Steve Fletcher against fellow relegation rivals Grimsby.

The Cherries had gone a goal behind, before Liam Feeney gave his side a lifeline. Before the packed-out crowd at Dean Court knew it, there was Supa Fletch to save the day and give Eddie Howe's side a huge three points.

That kit didn't have any red or black stripes down the front. It was a plain red colour, with flashes of black on the shoulders and at the back. It went down in history though, despite Fletch whipping it off in joy when wheeling away to celebrate his winner.

LEAGUE ONE PROMOTION

A Fila kit was worn for our promotion-winning season in League One, with the red and black stripes maintained for the home shirt. This is what we donned when we defeated Carlisle 3-1 to gain promotion to the Championship!

Steve Cook, Harry Arter and Brett Pitman all scored for the Cherries that day, with four players from the starting 11 still featuring for Eddie Howe's squad now!

CHAMPIONSHIP PROMOTION

Despite winning promotion against Bolton at Dean Court in the previous game, this kit was the one that we wore against Charlton at The Valley when we won the Championship title.

Two goals from Matt Ritchie, as well as another from Harry Arter gave the Cherries a 3-0 lead, with promotion rivals Watford only drawing to Sheffield Wednesday on the final day, meaning Eddie Howe's side had the title in the bag.

The blue and black fade on the kit was a big hit with supporters and was the club's third kit for the 2014/15 season. It will always go down as a famous strip due to it being the one that Tommy Elphick lifted the Championship trophy in.

FIRST PREMIER LEAGUE WIN

This season saw a change of sponsor and a change of kit supplier as the Cherries played their first season in the Premier League.

The away kit for the 2015/16 season had a similar theme to the third strip the previous year, which Eddie Howe's side had worn for that famous win at Charlton. Blue and black dominated throughout again, with a minor difference - the Premier League sleeve badges to mark the Cherries playing in the highest tier of English football.

This was the kit that we wore for our first ever Premier League win, a dramatic 4-3 victory over West Ham at Upton Park. It was one to remember for Callum Wilson, who stepped up to net his first hat-trick in the top flight!

CURRENT HOME KIT

Our latest home kit is one of the best, with dark red flashes showing on the Cherry red stripes! This one was made for the 2019/20 Premier League season, our fifth in English football's top flight. Even though we're wearing it in the current campaign, it actually had its first outing at the end of last season when Eddie Howe's side played Tottenham Hotspur in the final home game of the 2018/19 season.

It must have been a lucky one, as the Cherries recorded their first win over Spurs thanks to a header in the last minute from Nathan Ake. The visitors were down to nine men too, with Heung-Min Son and Juan Foyth both shown a red card during the game.

WHAT HAPPENS ON A
MATCHDAY

Aaron Ramsdale has played in plenty of matches in his young career so far, but how does he go about his business? We investigate...

09:00

The alarm goes off and I wake up, I'll then get up and have breakfast. It's usually something basic like a bottle of water and some toast.

09:25

After breakfast I'll have a shower, I might even go back to bed for a while or watch Soccer AM on the telly – I want to be as relaxed as possible on the morning of a game.

11:15

I live quite close to the stadium so it only takes about 10 minutes to get in. I drive in on my own and listen to my playlist in the car. There is absolutely everything on there. I've got every single genre from Elvis to Little Mix!

11:30

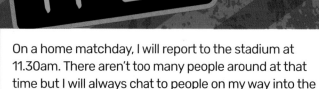

On a home matchday, I will report to the stadium at 11.30am. There aren't too many people around at that time but I will always chat to people on my way into the ground, if there are any fans who want autographs or selfies I will see them as well.

11:35

We normally head straight to the players' pavilion and sit down with all the other lads in the squad for pre-match food and then just chill, we're quite focussed at this point. If there's a lunchtime kick-off on Sky, we will sit down and watch the start of it.

12:50

We all walk back over to the changing rooms to start getting ready for the game.

1:30

We have a pre-match meeting in the physio's room and walk through set-plays, they're important for every single player, the finer details matter!

1:45

Everybody starts to get their gear on and have a stretch in the 3G area. Some people will do their own thing and I tend to stretch and get ready as the 'keepers warm up a little earlier at 2.05pm.

3:00

Kick-off!

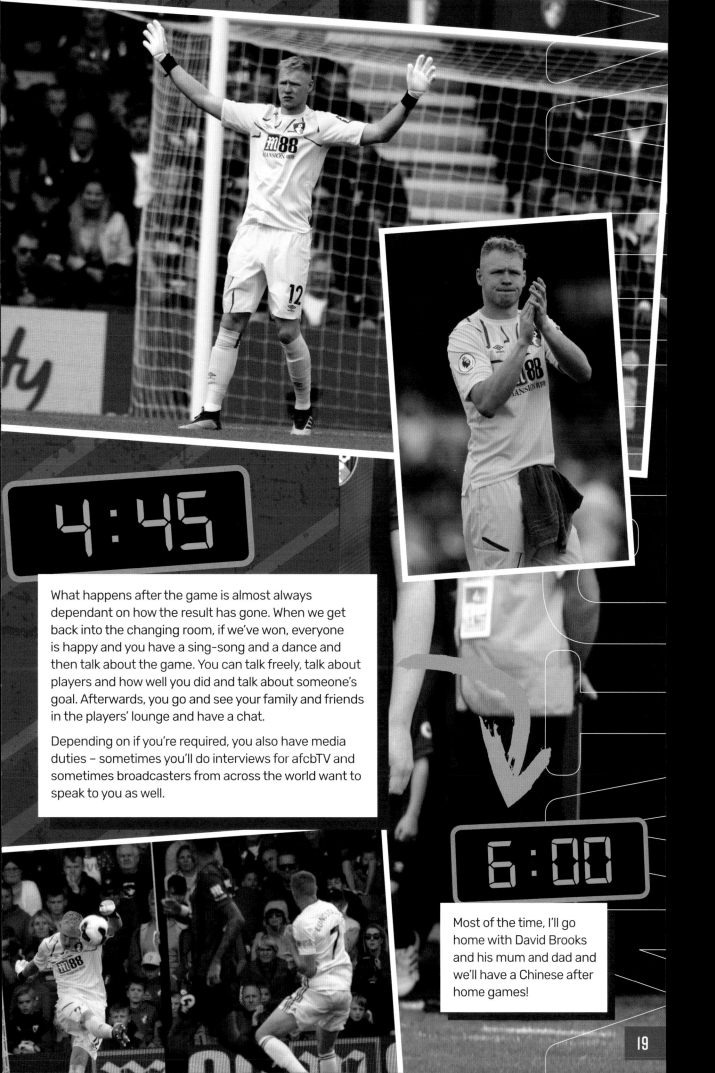

4:45

What happens after the game is almost always dependant on how the result has gone. When we get back into the changing room, if we've won, everyone is happy and you have a sing-song and a dance and then talk about the game. You can talk freely, talk about players and how well you did and talk about someone's goal. Afterwards, you go and see your family and friends in the players' lounge and have a chat.

Depending on if you're required, you also have media duties – sometimes you'll do interviews for afcbTV and sometimes broadcasters from across the world want to speak to you as well.

6:00

Most of the time, I'll go home with David Brooks and his mum and dad and we'll have a Chinese after home games!

SIMPLY
THE BEST

BEST PLAYER YOU'VE SEEN

Ronaldinho. He would play the game with a smile on his face and when I was younger, I would watch him on YouTube and try to recreate his skills and tricks! What a player he was.

ARNAUT
DANJUMA

BEST GOAL YOU'VE EVER SCORED

I've talked about this goal so much, it's definitely the one I scored in the Champions League against Atletico Madrid – I'm sure you know the one by now!

I just saw the opening and hit it from distance, it was my favourite one and I want to keep on scoring them for sure!

BEST GAME YOU'VE PLAYED IN

It's a tricky one, but I would have to say my international debut for Holland. Obviously it was a debut and of course that's the dream for any player. But we also beat Germany 3-0, and that doesn't happen often!

BEST CHILDHOOD MEMORY

This isn't football related.

I used to just love playing outside with my friends and I have some great memories doing that.

BEST FILM YOU'VE SEEN

Hmmmm... I'm not really a film guy, I like boxsets and *Game Of Thrones* is up there. But there was a film called The Equaliser with Denzil Washington – that's the one I'll go for!

BEST MEAL

Anything my parents cook for me, they're great cooks!

BEST BOOK YOU'VE READ

I did like the Zlatan autobiography, that was a really good read.

The other two for me would be Muhammed Ali and Mike Tyson's autobiographies, they were excellent. I think I'll have to go for Ali to be fair – the three of them are all interesting characters.

BEST APP YOU USE

WhatsApp. It keeps me in contact with everyone at home and I use it regularly to speak to people.

BURY 0 - 3 AFC BOURNEMOUTH
8TH AUGUST 2009

The Cherries hit the ground running by recording their first opening-day victory for 10 years.

Bury were among the favourites for promotion having lost out in the semi-final of the previous season's play-offs.

But first-half goals from Brett Pitman and Anton Robinson and a stunning strike from Mark Molesley after the break saw the Cherries demolish the Shakers at Gigg Lane.

AFC BOURNEMOUTH 1 - 0 BURTON ALBION
26TH SEPTEMBER 2009

Brett Pitman's wonder goal helped Eddie Howe's table-toppers carve a new chapter in the club's record books.

Pitman's sensational 25-yard volley earned the Cherries an eighth win in nine games – their best start to a season since they joined the Football League in 1923.

Due to a mounting injury crisis and an ongoing transfer embargo, manager Howe was only able to name three substitutes!

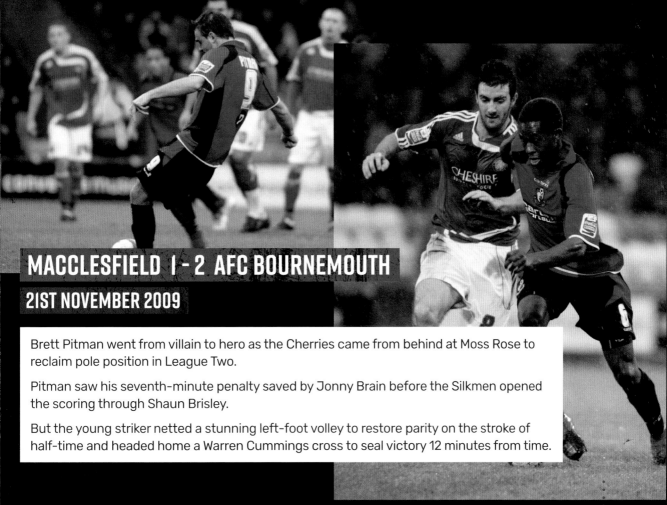

MACCLESFIELD 1 - 2 AFC BOURNEMOUTH

21ST NOVEMBER 2009

Brett Pitman went from villain to hero as the Cherries came from behind at Moss Rose to reclaim pole position in League Two.

Pitman saw his seventh-minute penalty saved by Jonny Brain before the Silkmen opened the scoring through Shaun Brisley.

But the young striker netted a stunning left-foot volley to restore parity on the stroke of half-time and headed home a Warren Cummings cross to seal victory 12 minutes from time.

CHELTENHAM 0 - 1 AFC BOURNEMOUTH

26TH DECEMBER 2009

Liam Feeney bagged the only goal as the Cherries got their promotion push back on track with a Boxing Day victory at Whaddon Road.

Feeney ended a four-month wait for a goal when he scored with a majestic strike 12 minutes into the second half.

It was the first goal scored by a Cherries player – with the exception of Brett Pitman – in more than 11 hours and left them in second place, five points behind leaders Rochdale.

CREWE 1 - 2 AFC BOURNEMOUTH
30TH JANUARY 2010

Steve Fletcher took centre stage as the Cherries halted a run of three successive defeats with a battling win at Gresty Road.

Fletcher headed home a Brett Pitman cross to open the scoring in the 21st minute and also had a hand in Anton Robinson's goal which doubled their lead after the break.

In a game which saw emergency loan signing Rhoys Wiggins make his debut following his move from Norwich, Luke Murphy halved the arrears three minutes after Robinson had scored.

NOTTS COUNTY 2 - 2 AFC BOURNEMOUTH
15TH MARCH 2010

Substitute Jeff Goulding came off the bench to grab a dramatic late equaliser in front of the Sky Sports cameras at Meadow Lane.

Goulding netted his first goal of an injury-interrupted season when he scored with a finely-taken volley from 12 yards in stoppage-time.

Fellow high-fliers Notts County, who had been seeking a fifth successive victory, twice took the lead through Lee Hughes with Goulding and Brett Pitman levelling for the Cherries.

BURTON ALBION 0 - 2 AFC BOURNEMOUTH
24TH APRIL 2010

Goals from Brett Pitman and Alan Connell saw Eddie Howe's heroes clinch promotion to League One following a two-year absence.

Pitman drew first blood with an excellent finish midway through the second half before Connell came off the bench to double their lead in the closing stages.

It marked the club's fifth promotion since they joined the Football League in 1923 – and easily the most remarkable following a campaign fraught with difficulty.

AFC BOURNEMOUTH 4 - 0 PORT VALE
1ST MAY 2020

Star striker Brett Pitman wrote his own piece of history as the Cherries brought down the curtain on their home campaign with a resounding win over the Valiants.

Pitman bagged his 28th goal of the season – and his 56th career strike – to join Luther Blissett in tenth place on the club's list of all-time leading scorers.

Substitute Alan Connell added a quickfire double and Josh McQuoid headed home to register his first career goal as the promotion party went into overdrive at Dean Court.

MY FAVOURITE MATCH

Being a professional footballer means you live and breathe the game. But what are some of our squad's favourite matches of all time?

CHRIS MEPHAM

I remember when I was younger, one of the games that stands out for me is the Champions League final in Istanbul, 2005.

Liverpool were 3-0 down as we all know and were written out of the game, they never looked like getting back into it.

I remember watching it with my dad and we were like 'wow this is unbelievable.' In a Champions League final to come back from that scoreline is incredible.

I've obviously watched loads of games since that day and for that one to stand up still to this day says a lot about it!

ARNAUT DANJUMA

That's such a tough one, I've played in a lot of games but I'll go for one that I watched as a kid.

It was 2006 and the World Cup was in Germany, I'll never forget the final that year.

France played Italy and my standout memory of that game was watching Zinedine Zidane.

In the first ten minutes, he had the bottle to dink a penalty past Ginaluigi Buffon. Dink one past him!

In a World Cup final!

Then obviously there was the Zidane headbutt and it went all the way to penalties, that's a game that I loved as a kid.

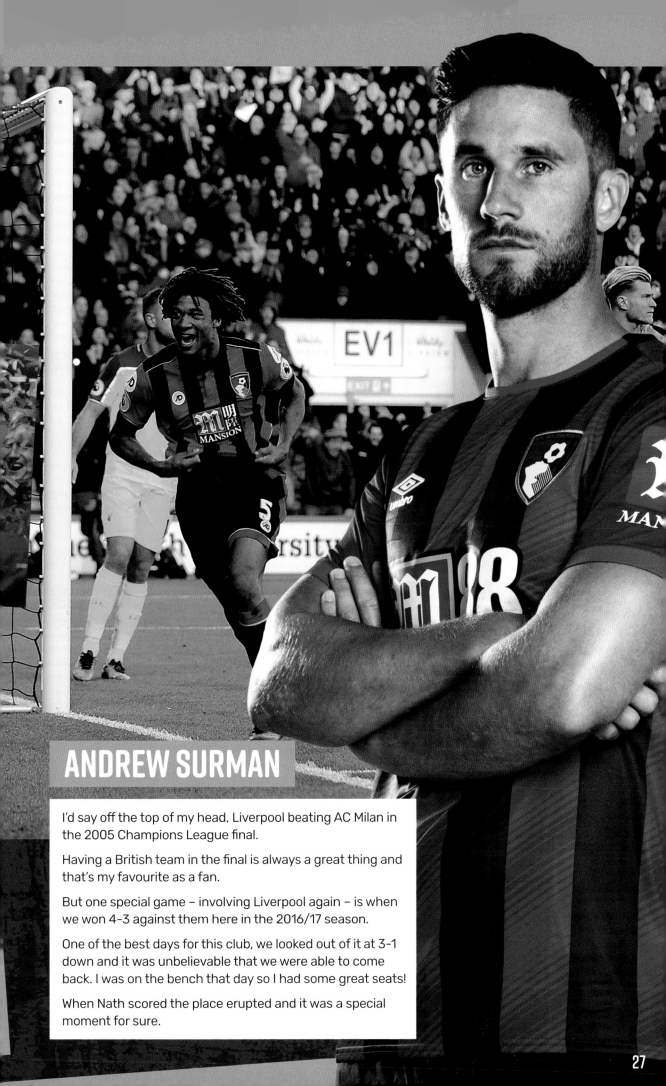

ANDREW SURMAN

I'd say off the top of my head, Liverpool beating AC Milan in the 2005 Champions League final.

Having a British team in the final is always a great thing and that's my favourite as a fan.

But one special game – involving Liverpool again – is when we won 4-3 against them here in the 2016/17 season.

One of the best days for this club, we looked out of it at 3-1 down and it was unbelievable that we were able to come back. I was on the bench that day so I had some great seats!

When Nath scored the place erupted and it was a special moment for sure.

DREAM TEAM

WITH WADE ELLIOTT

LB - WARREN CUMMINGS

Warren was brilliant with us and very good with me. He was a good player and a fantastic teammate and another one who would have played higher had it not been for injuries. We would always match up against each other in training and he helped develop my game.

CB - EDDIE HOWE

Eddie was a really good player. He was brave, he read the game well and was good on the ball. He wasn't the tallest defender in the world but he was very good in the air. He was always very composed and nothing ever seemed to faze him. It's no surprise to see him doing so well in management. He was our captain when he was 22 and was always a leader.

GOALKEEPER - NEIL MOSS

Neil was a big signing for us and I think we did really well to get him. He returned to the club in 2002/03 and played a major role in us winning promotion through the play-offs. He was solid and dependable and had a huge presence about him. He was steady and reliable and an all-round top goalkeeper.

CB - KARL BROADHURST

Karl was my roommate. He was a very underrated player and was an excellent out-and-out defender. You would want at least one of him in every squad. He was committed, whole-hearted and very determined. I am convinced he would have played at a much higher level had it not been for the bad injuries he suffered throughout his career.

Winger Wade Elliott was plucked from non-league Bashley in 2000 and went on to play more than 250 games for the Cherries alongside the likes of Eddie Howe and Steve Fletcher.

He starred in the club's 2003 Division Three play-off win over Lincoln at the Millennium Stadium before scoring the goal which took Burnley to the Premier League in 2009.

Elliott pipped ten-in-a-row striker Jermain Defoe to the Player of the Year award in 2000/01, the season that the Cherries got agonisingly close to making the Division Two play-offs.

Here, Elliott selects his favourite team from players he played with during his time at the club, a task he admitted was very difficult as there were so many to choose from.

RB - NEIL YOUNG

I made my debut with Neil and he virtually played it for me – he talked me through the whole game! We were a very young team and he seemed like one of the older heads, even though he was only about 25. He was a big character and took us under his wing. He was a great player as well. He could defend, get up and down the line and was always comfortable on the ball.

LM - GARRETH O'CONNOR

Garreth was probably one of the most talented players I played with at Bournemouth and had a great sense of humour. He was technically very good and we always dove-tailed quite well. I would stay really wide and try to open up the pitch which would buy a bit of space for him to come off the line and find pockets to play in. He scored some key goals during our promotion season.

CM - CARL FLETCHER

When I played with Carl, he had a couple of seasons in midfield and a couple at the back and was excellent in both positions which says everything you need to know about him as a player. He was a good footballer and a good captain. He was bright and tactically astute and it was no surprise to see him go on to play in the Premier League.

ST - STEVE FLETCHER

A legend! He has been brilliant for the club and was always great for me as a winger. You knew exactly what he wanted and you just had to put the ball in the box. If the cross was half-decent, there was always a chance he would get on the end of it. To this day, my greatest achievement in the game is getting him a hat-trick so I have to put him in my team just for that!

CM - BRIAN STOCK

We always used to link really well. He could find my feet or find me in behind. His range of passing helped make me a better player.

He epitomised the Bournemouth way of playing and you could always see he had the attributes to play at a higher level, which he did.

ST - JERMAIN DEFOE

He was just sensational when he came in on loan and it was ridiculous how good he was. I remember the first time he trained with us. It was at West Brom's training ground ahead of a game at Stoke. This little lad turned up and nobody had ever really heard of him then. But it took just one training session and you could see his class and quality, even when he had just turned 18. I have been fortunate to have played with some excellent strikers but, as a finisher, Jermain was the best I played with.

RM - JAMES HAYTER

James could play anywhere and was always a threat. He was a super player, really intelligent and razor sharp in front of goal. He's also one of the funniest people I have ever met. He didn't used to say too much but, when he did, it was always really funny. He was a brilliant player and someone you would always have in your team wherever you played him.

SUBSTITUTES - **GARETH STEWART, WARREN FEENEY, STEPHEN PURCHES, RICHARD HUGHES, MARK STEIN**

SIMPLY
THE BEST

BEST CHILDHOOD MEMORY

That's a hard one... This isn't from my childhood when I was really young, but when I got my scholarship at Brentford. I had so much disappointment in football and that was the moment that I had my confidence and belief back. That was a real turning point.

CHRIS
MEPHAM

BEST PLAYER YOU'VE SEEN LIVE

Another tough one! I remember one actually, it was Wales against Uruguay and I was on the bench.

Luis Suarez was playing and I remember just watching his movement, commanding his area and he was so impressive. He scored as well that day so he's up there!

BEST FOOTBALL SHIRT

I'd say the first time I put the Wales kit on, that is the best shirt to be fair – I like all of our kits at the club but that one has such a special occasion attached to it.

BEST MOMENT OF YOUR LIFE

Again this is probably not a unique answer! But I feel as a footballer your ambition should be to represent your country and my first start for Wales is the best moment so far.

BEST MEAL

If my mum is cooking, her Spaghetti Bolognese is top class.

BEST FILM YOU'VE SEEN

A classic – *The Godfather*, it's my and my dad's favourite film. Besides that, my favourite comedy is *Cool Runnings*.

BEST SOCIAL MEDIA PLATFORM

I use Instagram quite a lot. I like keeping up with all my friends and what they're getting up to, but it's also big for football. I like to see what my teammates post and it's definitely the one I use the most.

BEST STADIUM YOU'VE PLAYED AT

The Rose Bowl Stadium in Pasadena, California. It hosted the 1994 World Cup final and holds over 92,000 people. It was a massive arena and when I played it was full of Mexican people, a sell-out and that was my debut for Wales. Incredible.

Joshua King is our top scorer in the Premier League ever!

This is how the Norwegian frontman did it...

GOAL-
KING

GOAL 1 - SATURDAY 21ST NOVEMBER 2015
SWANSEA CITY 2-2 AFC BOURNEMOUTH

King's first ever Premier League goal came in a dramatic game at the Liberty Stadium.

Just ten minutes in, Junior Stanislas picked the ball up on the left-hand side of the box and he spotted King steaming into the middle.

The striker slid in to make great contact with Stanislas' pass to poke the ball past Lukasz Fabianski into the corner after just ten minutes. It was a sign of things to come for King!

GOAL 2 - SATURDAY 12TH DECEMBER 2015
AFC BOURNEMOUTH 2-1 MANCHESTER UNITED

In just three short months, King had written himself into Cherries folklore with one of the most memorable goals in the club's history.

Deadlocked with Louis van Gaal's Red Devils, a clever set play would pick the lock of the United defence.

Matt Ritchie swept in a low delivery which was dummied by Cherries' men in the middle, which allowed King – against his former club – to guide the ball into the bottom corner. Simply majestic!

GOAL 3 - SATURDAY 5TH MARCH 2016
NEWCASTLE UNITED 1-3 AFC BOURNEMOUTH

One of our finest away days!

After playing a big influence in forcing an own goal, King had a goal of his own in the second half – and some finish it was!

Some superb play from Lewis Grabban and Matt Ritchie saw the Scot pick out a superb pass. King turned really well, driving towards the Toon goal before slamming an unstoppable finish right in the top corner!

GOAL 4 - SATURDAY 9TH APRIL 2016
ASTON VILLA 1-2 AFC BOURNEMOUTH

A crucial game in our first Premier League season, as the victory against Villa meant we stayed in the league!

King showed he wasn't all about power on that day at Villa Park, when he nicked the ball right off Ciaran Clark's toe and showed the presence of mind to dink the ball over the on-rushing Brad Guzan into the corner.

It was a delightful chip and one that in the end rubber-stamped our Premier League status!

SWANSEA CITY 0-3 AFC BOURNEMOUTH

An absolutely clinical display from the Cherries at the Liberty Stadium.

With the score at 2-0, King replaced Ryan Fraser and was given 17 minutes to get in on the act.

Seconds were left on the clock when Charlie Daniels' through-ball found the striker and he reacted sharply to take an early shot past Lukasz Fabianski and into the bottom corner.

A superb finish!

GOAL 13 - SATURDAY 4TH MARCH 2017

MANCHESTER UNITED 1-1 AFC BOURNEMOUTH

Another game against Manchester United, another goal for our Norwegian frontman!

In a game probably more memorable for Tyrone Mings and Zlatan Ibrahimovic's incidents, at 1-0 down Marc Pugh won a penalty with a clever turn in the box.

King was given the responsibility. No Cherries player had ever scored at Old Trafford, but the Norwegian smashed his spot-kick right into the top corner past David de Gea.

Pressure? What pressure!?

GOAL 14, 15 & 16 - SATURDAY 11TH MARCH 2017

AFC BOURNEMOUTH 3-2 WEST HAM

A first Premier League hat-trick and one he'll never forget!

After missing a first-half penalty, Kingy scored one of the best goals of his career to make it 1-1.

He flicked the ball over Jose Fonte with one foot, before volleying the dropping ball into the bottom corner. Sensational!

Just after half-time, he then made it 2-1 with a close-range finish after making a clever run to the back post.

But the third and most important goal came with seconds left on the clock.

After a surging run by Marc Pugh, Jack Wilshere's shot was superbly saved by Darren Randolph. The ball then fell to King and time seemed to stand still with bodies in front of him - but he placed the ball right into the top corner and wheeled away to hug the manager to celebrate!

LIVERPOOL 2-2 AFC BOURNEMOUTH

Another late one!

With three minutes left, King was able to hold off the challenge of Ragnar Klavan, swivel and side-foot a precise effort into the corner.

King's late equaliser sparked scenes of joy in the away end as the strike secured a first-ever point at Anfield.

SUNDERLAND 0-1 AFC BOURNEMOUTH

King received a pass from Ryan Fraser to finish well in the area at the Stadium of Light.

Not only did the goal mean the Cherries passed the 40-point mark, but it also ended Sunderland's ten-year stay in the Premier League.

It was his 15th Premier League goal of a prolific season, he became only the second Norwegian to reach that number in a single campaign, following in the footsteps of Ole Gunnar Solskjaer who managed it in 2001/02!

20

BURNLEY 1-2 AFC BOURNEMOUTH

This one prompted commentator John Williams in the afcbTV commentary box to scream 'that's a great goal!'

King cut inside onto his right foot into the area and curled a sumptuous effort into the far corner giving England international Nick Pope no chance!

That was Premier League goal number 30 and took him 11 clear of anyone else.

29

35

WATFORD 0-4 AFC BOURNEMOUTH

Two goals for Kingy in one of our biggest ever Premier League wins!

The first was a coolly converted penalty which sent Ben Foster – who was having a great game – the wrong way.

The second was his only goal he's scored with his head for the club so far! Callum Wilson's brilliant cross was met by the Norwegian who had peeled to the back stick and deftly nodded into the corner.

32 & 33

35

GOAL 35 - SATURDAY 19TH JANUARY 2019

AFC BOURNEMOUTH 2-0 WEST HAM

A terrific goal more for its importance than its quality, with the Cherries looking to end a run of four straight Premier League defeats.

A goal up with minutes to go, it was a tense finish, until David Brooks squared the ball for King to finish past Lukasz Fabianski.

The strike meant that King had scored four goals and provided an assist in his three home league appearances against West Ham.

36 & 37

AFC BOURNEMOUTH 4-0 CHELSEA

What a night!

Two more goals came in one of the club's most amazing ever victories.

King had his first 90 seconds into the second half, smashing in Brooks' cut back, before Junior Stanislas picked out the striker's run and he sidefooted a superb effort past Kepa to make it 3-0!

39 & 40

AFC BOURNEMOUTH 2-2 NEWCASTLE UTD

Another brace for King and another excellent strike to go with it.

The first was a penalty to equalise, before Dominic Solanke produced some superb footwork in the box. That allowed him to lay the ball off to King to curl a magnificent effort into the bottom corner to send the home fans into elation.

A superb finish!

Christmas

WITH ANDREW SURMAN

The festive period is a chance for everyone to let their hair down and enjoy some great food and company. But how does it differ for a footballer?

Vice-captain Andrew Surman reveals all!

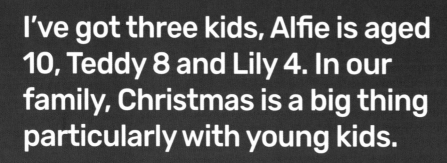

"
I've got three kids, Alfie is aged 10, Teddy 8 and Lily 4. In our family, Christmas is a big thing particularly with young kids.
"

We train on Christmas Eve and then I go home and help set everything up for the big day.

We play games the night before, set out the carrots and cake for Father Christmas and we're in a good routine now, we're lucky that the gaffer gives us Christmas Day off, that doesn't happen at a lot of clubs.

Our usual day is that we wake up really early in the morning and open presents with the kids. We usually host Christmas at our house so all of our family can come together. It's all about the kids and of course the difficult side of things as a player is everyone is letting their hair down, but you can't relax as your mind is also on Boxing Day.

While everyone else may snack, pick at things and have a big dinner, I have to have my three meals a day to be in the best shape possible for Boxing Day. I can't have any chocolate or anything like that and I wouldn't want to, as I don't want to feel heavy on Boxing Day.

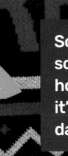

Sometimes on Christmas Day we will travel in the evening so we may leave at 6pm, but I'm lucky enough to still be home for Christmas. Lots of teams will train and travel so it's not too much different to normal. The kids have a great day and I'm there to see it and that's the main thing.

TO

1 AFC Bournemouth's only Wembley final was in 1998, the Auto Windscreens Shield defeat to Grimsby Town.

2 The Cherries have won two league titles – the Championship in 2014/15 and the Third Division in 1986/87.

3 Callum Wilson scored AFC Bournemouth's first hat-trick in the Premier League during a 4-3 win at West Ham in August 2015.

4 Eddie Howe's team won four Premier League games in succession in 2018 – Swansea (1-0), Burnley (2-1), Cardiff (2-0), West Ham (2-1).

5 The Cherries spent five seasons in the second flight and are currently in their fifth year in the top flight.

6 Junior Stanislas' double and goals from Charlie Daniels, Steve Cook, Callum Wilson and Dan Gosling saw AFC Bournemouth score six goals for the first time in the Premier League against Hull City in October 2016.

7 The Cherries have been promoted on seven occasions – 1971, 1982, 1987, 2003, 2010, 2013 and 2015.

8 In the 2009/10 League Two promotion campaign, AFC Bournemouth won eight of their first nine league games, the club's best start to a season since joining the Football League in 1923.

9 Ted MacDougall hit nine goals in an 11-0 win against Margate in the first round of the FA Cup in November 1971 – still an individual goalscoring record for the competition proper.

10 In 2000/01, Jermain Defoe, who was on loan from West Ham, scored in ten Division Two games on the trot for the Cherries.

11 Charlie Daniels has taken squad number 11 ever since he joined the Cherries permanently in January 2012.

MY FAVOURITE MATCH

We asked some of the lads to tell us their favourite match that they either watched or played in. Here's what they said...

CHARLIE DANIELS

My favourite game so far has been Newcastle away when we won 3-1 in our first Premier League season.

We were in the pink kit and growing up I was a Newcastle supporter so to score in a game like that and play at St James' Park for the first time, was incredible.

For us it was a great win at the time, we were 2-1 up and they were on top and it was a bit backs against the wall. I played a one-two with Pughie, luckily I then shot and it went into the bottom corner, so that was my favourite game so far!

RYAN FRASER

It's not one I've watched, so this is just a personal one for me.

It was the Arsenal home game in 2016/17, when we went 3-0 up, Charlie scored the first, Callum scored a penalty before I got the third.

It was such an unbelievable performance, in the second half I got the ball down the left-hand side off Hector Bellerin, and I put the ball under Petr Cech and scored.

Unfortunately we went on to draw the game 3-3, when you're 3-0 up that's always disappointing.

But from a purely personal perspective, I was pleased with my performance in that game and it was one of my first Premier League games so it sticks in the memory.

LEWIS COOK

My favourite game was Chelsea away when we won 3-0, I think that's all I need to say!

I think it was just because we were playing one of the bigger teams, playing away and the performance that we put in was one of high intensity, it was one of the best since I've been at the club.

Scoring three goals at a place like that is great. I think collectively as a team and for myself personally, we played really well and the celebrations in the changing room after the game were really good and stick in my memory.

JACK SIMPSON

For me it would have to be the Spurs home game from last season. Obviously to beat a team like that, it was a big achievement and it was the first time we'd beaten them in the Premier League so it was great to achieve that.

Also we were in the new kit, it was the last home game of the season so it was a big game for us to end on and we wanted to end on a high.

To do it in the way we did with a last minute winner, there's not really a better feeling in football than that. There were a lot of photos of me and Nathan Ake flying around after which were quite funny, so that one definitely has to go down as my favourite game.

SIMPLY
THE BEST

BEST PLAYER YOU'VE SEEN LIVE

I would say Hazard, but he pipped me with his assists last season! No, I would honestly say Hazard and over the last four or five years I've watched him a lot and I've learned a lot from him. I remember him having a season where he didn't score too many, but he came back so well.

RYAN
FRASER

BEST CHERRIES MOMENT

Arsenal at home, I think. I scored and got an assist, and we were unlucky not to win the game. We were actually 3-0 up and Franno got sent off! But I would say that one on a personal note.

BEST PLAYER YOU'VE PLAYED WITH

Away from our team - Andrew Robertson. I play with him for Scotland and he's unbelievable. He's our captain now too.

BEST FOOTBALL SHIRT

Probably a Scotland one because I used to be in the Scotland fan club and go to all the games. I used to pay my monthly subscription, so that's why I would say a Scotland one, any one.

BEST FILM YOU'VE EVER SEEN

The Dark Knight, I'm a big fan!

BEST THING ABOUT SCOTLAND

The golf courses. They've got the best ones, they're always green and they always look so picturesque. They're nice down here too, but they're nowhere near as good as in Scotland.

BEST BOOK YOU'VE READ

Pep Guardiola's biography by Guillem Balague. It's very good and well worth a read.

BEST MEAL

Wagamama! Chicken Katsu Curry is my favourite without a doubt!

BEST STADIUM YOU'VE PLAYED AT

Old Trafford! It's just as nice as it looks in the photos.

ALL-TIME
AFC BOURNEMOUTH

DREAM TEAM

Pick your favourite 11 from AFC Bournemouth's best ever players, choose wisely!

TOMMY GODWIN

SEASONS: 1952-1962

Born in Dublin, Godwin came to England with Leicester City and three years later joined the Cherries for a ten-year stint, keeping out plenty of shots on the south coast.

He was a key man in the legendary 1957 FA Cup quarter-final run and was the Cherries' first ever international, playing a total of 13 times for the Republic of Ireland.

NEIL MOSS

SEASONS: 1993-1995 & 2003-2008

From the local area, Moss was between the sticks for the Cherries while he was still a teenager, before moving along the coast to Southampton.

Aged 28, the 'keeper came back again and had a hugely successful time back with the club. He won promotion with us in 2003 at the Millennium Stadium in the famous win over Lincoln and even played in 115 consecutive matches at one point!

ARTUR BORUC

SEASONS: 2014-PRESENT

The big Pole in our goal came on loan as we romped to the Championship, an important player for the club as we pushed towards the top flight – and his influence meant we made sure we signed him permanently as we got set for our first Premier League season.

Be it saving big penalties at Old Trafford or commanding his area, Boruc has penned his name in Bournemouth history and is still going strong as he approaches his 40th birthday!

DAVID JAMES

SEASONS: 2012-2013

An FA Cup and League Cup winner with over 50 caps for England, James was a big signing when he came to the Cherries towards the end of his career, and he still had plenty to give playing for us for a season when he was in his 40s.

Earlier in his career, the giant stopper played for Liverpool and Manchester City and was at one time the Premier League player with the most appearances and the 'keeper with the most clean sheets.

GERRY PEYTON

SEASONS: 1986-1991

In the second half of the 1980s Peyton was a great 'keeper for Harry Redknapp's Cherries as they got to the second tier for the first time ever and stayed there for two seasons.

The Ireland international played every game in the promotion winning season in 1986/87 before moving on to Everton, and is now a goalkeeping coach in Japan after doing the same job for big guns Arsenal.

GOALKEEPERS

GOALKEEPERS   BEST OF THE REST

ASMIR BEGOVIC

VINCE BARTRAM

KEN BIRD

SHAWN JALAL

DAVID BEST

47

DEFENDERS

TOMMY ELPHICK

SEASONS: 2012-2016

A true leader, the former Brighton centre-back was instrumental in the team getting promoted to the Premier League, becoming a legend as captain as the Cherries won the Championship in 2014/15!

NATHAN AKE

SEASONS: 2016-PRESENT

The classy Dutch centre-back has been so consistent since joining the club permanently from Chelsea in 2017.

He's been an ever-present in his two permanent Premier League seasons at the club with his calmness and quality of passing out from the back trademarks of his game.

STEVE COOK

SEASONS: 2011-PRESENT

Cook's importance has only continued to grow seven years after he first joined the club on loan from Brighton.

Not only has the centre-back progressed through the leagues with the club, he's become a rock in the Premier League and surpassed 300 league appearances for the club last season!

PAUL MORRELL

SEASONS: 1983-1993

Legendary full-back Morrell not only played well over 400 times for the club, but he scored the winning goal in the first Football League Trophy Final - then known as the Associate Members' Cup - in the 2-1 win over Hull City 2-1 at Boothferry Park in 1984.

BEST OF THE REST

DEFENDERS

ADAM SMITH

JOHN WILLIAMS

JASON PEARCE

RYAN GARRY

SHAUN TEALE

SEASONS: 1989-1991

The centre-back joined the club from Weymouth in 1989 for £50,000 and what a bargain it proved to be!

He spent three years at Vitality Stadium, making 100 league appearances and he was that good he went to help Aston Villa become Premier League runners-up!

SIMON FRANCIS

SEASONS: 2011-PRESENT

Our club captain, Francis' leadership is hailed by both supporters and players.

His impact as both a centre-back in his later years and a right-back can't be underestimated and the towering defender has made over 300 appearances during the club's rise.

EDDIE HOWE

SEASONS: 1994-2002 & 2004-2007

One word to describe the manager when he was a player – classy.

Coming through the ranks at Vitality Stadium, he had two separate spells making over 250 league appearances and was that popular with the fans they grouped together to fund his return to the club in 2004!

NEIL YOUNG

SEASONS: 1994-2008

Young played over 500 games for the club after joining in 1994 from Tottenham Hotspur.

He spent 14 years at the Cherries and became a club hero with his committed displays from right full-back.

WARREN CUMMINGS

SEASONS: 2000-2012

After two successful loan spells, Scottish defender Cummings signed for the club in 2003 and enjoyed an unbelievable nine-year spell.

The left-back saw it all in his time with the club and was the life and soul in the dressing room at Vitality Stadium.

DEFENDERS

DEFENDERS

BEST OF THE REST

IAN COX

CHARLIE DANIELS

SHAUN COOPER

JOHN IMPEY

CENTRAL

STEPHEN PURCHES

SEASONS: **2000-2007 & 2010-2014**

A versatile performer during his two spells with the Cherries, Purches played 277 league games for the club before retiring in May 2014.

He finished off a sweeping team move to score a memorable goal during the 2003 League Two play-off final against Lincoln and helped the club reach the 2010/11 League One play-offs.

LEWIS COOK

SEASONS: **2016-PRESENT**

A graduate of the Leeds United academy, Cook joined the Cherries in July 2016 and captained England to glory during the 2017 Under-20 World Cup and the 2018 Toulon Tournament.

Since his arrival at Vitality Stadium, the gifted playmaker has impressed supporters with his silky skills and fine displays and won his first cap for England in March 2018.

DANNY HOLLANDS

SEASONS: **2006-2011**

Signed from Chelsea in July 2006, the industrious and hard-working midfielder was voted supporters' player of the year in 2007/08.

He starred in the 2008/09 Greatest Escape campaign and again when the Cherries won promotion to League One the following season.

HARRY ARTER

SEASONS: **2010-PRESENT**

A bargain £4,000 buy from non-league Woking in July 2010, Arter has played a pivotal role in the club's rise from the depths of League One to the Premier League.

The Republic of Ireland international turned in a series of outstanding displays and was a regular when Eddie Howe's team won the Championship in 2014/15.

IAN BISHOP

SEASONS: **1988-1989**

Creative and skilful, Bishop made a huge impression on the Cherries supporters despite spending just one season at the club.

Signed for a bargain £35,000 from Carlisle in July 1988, Bishop starred as the Cherries finished 12th in the second tier, a club record before the Eddie Howe era.

BEST OF THE REST — CENTRAL MIDFIELDERS

ANTON ROBINSON

BRIAN STOCK

RICHARD HUGHES

KEITH MILLER

SEAN O'DRISCOLL

JEFFERSON LERMA

SEASONS: **2018-PRESENT**

Capped his first year at the club by winning the goal of the season for his stunning 30-yarder on the final day of 2018/19 in the 5-3 defeat at Crystal Palace.

The Colombia international has made a big impression on the Cherries supporters and has turned in a series of wholehearted displays in the Premier League.

MATT HOLLAND

SEASONS: **1995-1997**

Voted supporters' player of the season in 1995/96, Holland was a hugely popular figure at Dean Court after signing as a relative unknown from West Ham in January 1995.

He played a key role during the second half of the 1994/95 Great Escape season and went on to become an inspirational club captain.

ANDREW SURMAN

SEASONS: **2005-2006 & 2013-PRESENT**

Enjoyed two fruitful loan spells with the Cherries before signing permanently in August 2014.

A key player as the club clinched promotion by winning the Championship in 2014/15, Surman has also featured prominently in the Premier League.

STEVE ROBINSON

SEASONS: **1994-2000**

Signed from Tottenham in October 1994, Robinson scored 60 goals in 286 appearances before joining Preston in May 2000.

An assured penalty-taker, he starred in the 1994/95 Great Escape season and also played in the 1998 Auto Windscreens Shield final at Wembley.

CARL FLETCHER

SEASONS: **1997-2004**

Fletcher graduated through the Cherries youth ranks to become one of the most influential players in the club's recent history.

He skippered the team to glory in the 2003 League Two play-off final after being voted supporters' player of the year in the same season.

MIDFIELDERS

CENTRAL MIDFIELDERS

BEST OF THE REST

TONY PULIS

DARREN ANDERTON

EUNAN O'KANE

DAN GOSLING

GAVIN PEACOCK

WINGERS

RONNIE BOLTON

SEASONS: 1958-1965 & 1967-1969

Over half a century ago Bolton came through the ranks as a pro with the Cherries and was soon showing what he could do in the first team, with plenty of goals to his game as well as his strong work out wide.

Bolton played across two spells for the club, during the first spell he led the Cherries in goalscoring – including an incredible overhead kick against Shrewsbury – and nearly securing promotion before returning after two years away with Ipswich.

RYAN FRASER

SEASONS: 2013-PRESENT

Fraser was just a teenager when he arrived on the south coast from Aberdeen in Scotland, and what a player he has become for the Cherries in the Premier League!

Wee Man has become stronger and his ability has gone through the roof, becoming a big threat to opposition defences with both his goalscoring and assists – last season only Eden Hazard got more assists in the Premier League than Fraser!

WADE ELLIOTT

SEASONS: 2001-2005

Released by Southampton as a teenager, it didn't seem like Elliott would make it, until he was spotted by the Cherries, started training with the club and was finally a footballer when he became a Cherries man aged 21.

What a spot Elliott was! Player of the year in his first full season, for five years he was a rampaging force down the flank for the side, chipping in with his share of goals before heading up the divisions to join Burnley and eventually playing with them in the Premier League.

JOHN BAILEY

SEASONS: 1995-2000

The Cherries have been around for over 120 years now, but Bailey is still the only player who's scored for us at Wembley. That was back in 1998 when we reached the home of English football for the first time in the Auto Windscreens Final.

Bailey was tigerish and never let the opposition have an easy afternoon with his wing work, but after five years at the club a back injury sadly brought an early end to his career.

MARC PUGH

SEASONS: 2010-2019

What a journey Pugh went on with the club! Joining the Cherries after promotion to League One, his trickery down the wing left many a defender bamboozled and he was the Cherries' top scorer in his first season.

In nearly a decade with the club Pughie won promotion twice, helped us stay in the Premier League and scored the first hat-trick of his career in the incredible 8-0 win at Birmingham City back in the Championship.

BEST OF THE REST

WINGERS

MATT RITCHIE

MARK MOLESLEY

DAVID BROOKS

RUSSELL BEARDSMORE

LIAM FEENEY

BRETT PITMAN

SEASONS: 2005-2010 & 2012-2015

Crowned supporters' player of the year in 2009/10, Jerseyman Pitman's 96 goals make him the club's fourth all-time leading league marksman.

His goals were crucial in the club's rapid rise from the depths of League Two to the Premier League.

TED MACDOUGALL

SEASONS: 1969-1972 & 1978-1980

SuperMac plundered 144 goals in 223 games across two spells at AFC Bournemouth, including a record nine-goal haul in an FA Cup first-round win over Margate in 1971.

He hit 42 league goals to spearhead the Cherries' promotion from Division Four in 1970/71 and was leading goalscorer for three seasons on the trot between 1969/70 and 1971/72.

JAMES HAYTER

SEASONS: 1997-2007

A product of the club's youth ranks, Hayter notched 94 goals in 358 league games and played a key role in the Cherries' 2002/03 Division Three play-off final triumph against Lincoln City.

He hit the headlines when he scored three times in 140 seconds in a 6-0 win over Wrexham in February 2004 – the fastest hat-trick in the history of the Football League.

RON EYRE

SEASONS: 1925-1933

The Cherries' all-time record goalscorer, Eyre netted 229 times in 337 appearances in all competitions between January 1925 and May 1933.

He was the club's leading marksman in eight successive seasons and starred as the Cherries took eventual winners Bolton Wanderers to an FA Cup fourth-round replay in 1925/26.

CALLUM WILSON

SEASONS: 2014-PRESENT

Free-scoring Wilson netted 20 times in 45 league games as the Cherries won the Championship and secured promotion to the Premier League in 2014/15.

He has taken the step up in his stride and scored regularly in the top flight as well as winning international recognition with England.

STRIKERS

STRIKERS

BEST OF THE REST

JOSHUA KING

JERMAIN DEFOE

STEVE FLETCHER

STEVE JONES

COLIN CLARKE

ALL-TIME

You've seen the best AFC Bournemouth have
to offer, now choose your dream XI wisely!

GOALKEEPER

CENTRE-BACK

CENTRE-BACK

FULL-BACK

FULL-BACK

CENTRE MIDFIELD

CENTRE MIDFIELD

WINGER

WINGER

STRIKER

STRIKER

THREE SUBSTITUTES

AFC BOURNEMOUTH

DREAM TEAM

INTERNATIONAL INTELLECT

It's a difficult one, but how many of these questions can you answer on some of our internationals – without using Google?

1. Nathan Ake has over five caps for the Netherlands national team. True or false?

....

2. Against which country did Chris Mepham make his international debut?

....

3. Callum Wilson scored his first England goal last season, but against which country?

....

4. In what year did Joshua King make his first appearance for Norway – 2010, 2012 or 2014?

....

5. How many times did Jefferson Lerma play in the Copa America 2019 – two, three or four?

....

6. David Brooks' first international goal came against Slovakia. True or false?

....

7. How many times has Lewis Cook played for the senior England team? Once, twice or three times.

....

8. Arnaut Danjuma made his debut against Germany, but what was the final score in that game?

....

Answers on Page 62

QUIZ TIME   55

ANAGRAM CORNER

We've muddled these players' names up to make it hard for you to guess them... see how long it takes you to unravel them!

CURATOR RUB

....

COLUMNA WILLS

....

ASSISTOR JULIANN

....

DONICA MOLESKIN

....

CHIMP MASHER

....

GLIB HILL IP PIN

....

COKES VOTE

....

FRAY SNARER

....

PLAYER ONE

Clue One: One of my previous clubs is Luton Town.
Clue Two: I used to play as a winger as a child!
Clue Three: I scored in pre-season!

....

PLAYER TWO

Clue One: I'm a midfielder who can also play in defence.
Clue Two: I used to play for Tottenham!
Clue Three: I played for Nigeria at the U20 World Cup.

....

PLAYER THREE

Clue One: I joined the club back in 2014.
Clue Two: I've played for Newcastle United.
Clue Three: I scored once last season.

....

WHO AM I?

CHERRIES CROSSWORD

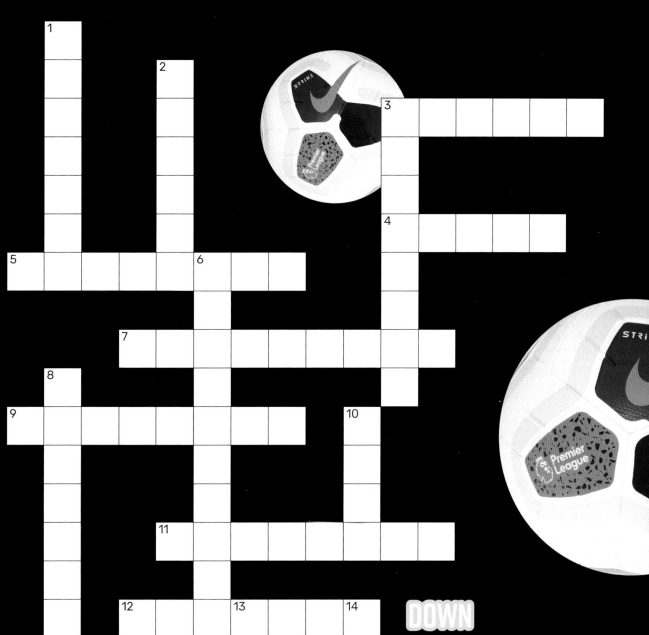

ACROSS

3. Our first ever England goalscorer
4. Joshua King's squad number
5. *I'm A Celebrity* winner and former manager
7. Ground where we won our first ever Premier League game
9. Young Irishman who scored against Lyon in pre-season
11. Club legend who scored that crucial goal against Grimsby
12. Club captain

DOWN

1. The club we signed Jefferson Lerma from
2. Legendary goal-getter who moved on to Ipswich and Portsmouth
3. West Ham midfielder and former Cherry
6. The first team we ever played against in the Premier League
8. Our assistant manager
10. Cherries legend now at QPR
13. Our highest ever placed finish
14. Diego Rico's country

NAME THE TEAM

Can you name all of the players in these team photos?

1 .... 2 .... 3 ....

4 .... 5 .... 6 ....

7 .... 8 .... 9 ....

WORDSEARCH

Hidden in the wordsearch below are the names of 20 AFC Bournemouth players, can you find them all? Words go horizontally, vertically, and backwards.

G	N	I	K	L	L	R	S	B	L	E	R	M	A
N	S	F	S	V	T	I	T	R	A	V	E	R	S
C	M	R	I	N	H	C	O	O	K	O	E	S	I
I	E	A	M	R	S	O	K	O	T	S	B	T	O
V	P	N	P	S	M	I	I	K	L	E	I	A	S
O	H	C	S	S	I	B	A	S	D	E	K	N	E
G	A	I	O	A	T	E	R	G	A	M	S	I	K
E	M	S	N	I	H	L	E	O	N	K	L	S	N
B	A	A	Y	E	C	A	T	S	J	J	E	L	A
K	E	K	A	S	M	D	S	L	U	E	I	A	L
R	H	E	E	S	A	S	G	I	M	C	N	S	O
R	S	V	L	S	L	M	L	N	A	E	A	L	S
V	R	C	B	M	I	A	R	G	A	S	D	A	H
E	E	A	M	J	S	R	N	L	G	B	B	Y	T

AKE	BEGOVIC	BROOKS	COOK	DANIELS
DANJUMA	FRANCIS	GOSLING	IBE	KING
LERMA	MEPHAM	RAMSDALE	RICO	SIMPSON
SMITH	SOLANKE	STACEY	STANISLAS	TRAVERS

SQUAD NUMBER CONUNDRUM

Can you do the maths to work out these squad numbers?

1. Joshua King's squad number + Dan Gosling's squad number x Simon Francis' number =

....

2. Andrew Surman's number x Steve Cook's number – Nathan Ake's number =

....

3. Lloyd Kelly's number + Philip Billing's number divided by Charlie Daniels' number =

....

4. Kyle Taylor's number – Jack Simpson's number =

....

5. David Brooks' number + Artur Boruc's number =

....

6. Jefferson Lerma's number + Joshua King's number =

....

VITALITY STADIUM QUIZ

1. How many seats are in the Colmar Construction Ted MacDougall stand - 2,000, 2,200 or 2,400?

....

2. What year was the ground rebuilt, 2000, 2001 or 2002?

....

3. Vitality Stadium is the only ground in the Premier League to have less than 20,000 seats. True or false?

....

4. When did the stadium first open, 1910, 1980 or 1993?

....

5. Our record attendance is over 28,000. True or false?

....

A1	A2	A3	A4	A5	A6	A7
B1	B2	B3	B4	B5	B6	B7
C1	C2	C3	C4	C5	C6	C7
D1	D2	D3	D4	D5	D6	D7
E1	E2	E3	E4	E5	E6	E7
F1	F2	F3	F4	F5	F6	F7
G1	G2	G3	G4	G5	G6	G7
H1	H2	H3	H4	H5	H7

INTERNATIONAL INTELLECT

1. True
2. Mexico
3. USA
4. 2012
5. Two
6. False
7. Once
8. 3-0

NAME THE TEAM

1. Gavin Kilkenny
2. Diego Rico
3. Nnamdi Ofoborh
4. Philip Billing
5. Joshua King
6. Jack Stacey
7. Mark Travers
8. Jefferson Lerma
9. Jordon Ibe

ANAGRAM CORNER

CURATOR RUB = ARTUR BORUC
COLUMNA WILLS = CALLUM WILSON
ASSISTOR JULIANN = JUNIOR STANISLAS
DONICA MOLESKIN = DOMINIC SOLANKE
CHIMP MASHER = CHRIS MEPHAM
GLIB HILL IP PIN = PHILIP BILLING
COKES VOTE = STEVE COOK
FRAY SNARER = RYAN FRASER

WORDSEARCH

G	N	I	K	L	L	R	S	B	L	E	R	M	A
N	S	F	S	V	T	I	T	R	A	V	E	R	S
C	M	R	I	N	H	C	O	O	K	O	E	S	I
I	E	A	M	R	S	O	K	O	T	S	B	T	O
V	P	N	P	S	M	I	I	K	L	E	I	A	S
O	H	C	S	S	I	B	A	S	D	E	K	N	E
G	A	I	O	A	T	E	R	G	A	M	S	I	K
E	M	S	N	I	H	L	E	O	N	K	L	S	N
B	A	A	Y	E	C	A	T	S	J	J	E	L	A
K	E	K	A	S	M	D	S	L	U	E	I	A	L
R	H	E	E	S	A	S	G	I	M	C	N	S	O
R	S	V	L	S	L	M	L	N	A	E	A	L	S
V	R	C	B	M	I	A	R	G	A	S	D	A	H
E	E	A	M	J	S	R	N	L	G	B	B	Y	T

SPOT THE BALL

H2

SQUAD NUMBER CONUNDRUM

1. Harry Wilson - 22
2. Callum Wilson - 13
3. Nathan Ake - 5
4. Steve Cook - 3
5. Diego Rico - 21
6. Adam Smith - 15

CHERRIES CROSSWORD

Down
1. Levante
2. Pitman
3. Wilshere
6. Aston Villa
8. Tindall
10. Pugh
13. Ninth
14. Spain

Across
3. Wilson
4. Seven
5. Redknapp
7. Upton Park
9. Kilkenny
11. Fletcher
12. Francis

VITALITY STADIUM QUIZ

1. 2,400
2. 2001
3. True
4. 1910
5. True

WHO AM I?

1. Jack Stacey
2. Nnamdi Ofoborh
3. Dan Gosling